T0398438

The FRIENDSHIP GUIDE

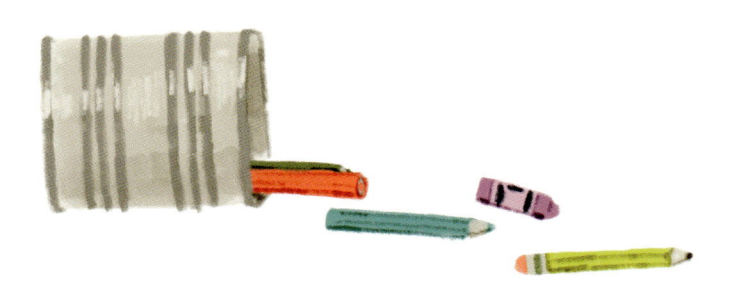

The
FRIENDSHIP
GUIDE

Dr. Jillian Roberts

Illustrated by
Andrea Armstrong

ORCA BOOK PUBLISHERS

Friendship is a huge part of life.

Friends help us when we need them and give us hugs when we're having a bad day. They're good listeners who know our deepest secrets and our biggest dreams. And, best of all, they make us laugh.

But friendship isn't just about getting. It's about giving too. It's kind of like a teeter-totter—you each need to do your part or it just isn't fun.

The golden rule of friendship is

You need to be a good friend yourself.

Being a good friend isn't always easy, though—it's a skill. And you get better the more you practice. But how? Read on for some great tips on how to be the best friend you can be.

**A great friend thinks of other people,
not just themselves.**

At recess Adelaide wants to play on the swings, and so does her friend Selma. But there's only one swing left. Adelaide wants to grab the swing for herself...

...but she decides to let Selma go first. It's not easy, but it feels good to be nice. Plus, Selma doesn't take too long, so Adelaide has time to swing before recess ends. Everybody wins!

YOUR TURN

What would you do in this situation? There isn't just one right answer—there are lots of ways to be a good friend. As you read this book, try to think of other ways you might respond. Maybe you have better ideas!

Friends are patient and kind, and they try not to be mean.

Mateo invites Samantha over for a playdate. He hopes they can ride their scooters to the park. But Samantha just got hers, and she's still really wobbly. Mateo speeds past her...

...but when he looks back and sees her struggling, he slows down. Then he rides alongside her till they get there. It wouldn't be fun at the park without her anyway.

SAYING SORRY

We all say or do not-great things sometimes. Even to friends. Just remember you can always say you're sorry. Friends forgive you if you've made a mistake.

Friends know the difference between right and wrong and help others be their best selves.

It's Sofia's birthday party, and her cake is Reza's favorite—chocolate fudge. So he even takes a second piece. But uh-oh. Sofia wants more too, and now there's none left. Reza's about to take a bite...

...but he puts down his fork and offers his piece to her. Sofia smiles, and they make a deal. They'll split it—and get some extra ice cream and candy on the side.

WHAT IS FAIR?

It's easy for a person getting the worse deal to see that something's not fair. It takes a special person to recognize that they're the lucky one and then help someone else.

Friends welcome newcomers into their group.

Reena is new to class, and she doesn't have any friends yet. Marisol and Hae-Won notice her sitting by herself at lunch, reading a book. At first they think maybe she wants to be alone...

...but Hae-Won asks her to sit with them, just in case. Reena smiles and comes right over. It turns out she is just shy, and she's happy to have new friends to talk to.

IT'S NOT EASY BEING NEW
You don't always have to make a big gesture. Just saying hi or smiling at someone new can make all the difference.

Friends share and invite others to play with them.

JP and Ichiro have been going to the same summer camp for years, and they know the routine. But this is Luna's first year there, so at playtime she's late getting to the toys. JP and Ichiro look at Luna's bent Hula-Hoop...

...and offer to share their toys with her. They also ask Luna to sit with them at craft time. Showing her around makes them feel special and helps Luna out too.

MAKING ROOM
Sometimes you might just want to hang out with your besties, but on other days, try including others who haven't found a friend group yet. Who knows—they might end up being really cool!

Friends don't call each other names or tease, and they stick up for kids being bullied.

After school Joaquin and Reese walk past some older kids teasing a kindergarten girl. Some of those kids are pretty big, and Joaquin and Reese don't want to get picked on themselves. But the girl looks really scared. Even though they're nervous...

...Joaquin and Reese decide to help. They track down a teacher and wait until she gets the older kids to move along. Then they stick around until the little girl's dad shows up, to make sure she's okay.

BULLIES

Dealing with bullying can be hard and complicated. If you notice bullying happening but don't feel safe standing up to the bully yourself, ask an adult for help.

Good friends are open to others' ideas and don't just play what they want to play.

Ella, Pria and Devon are hanging out at the park.
"Let's pretend we're warriors, defending a castle!" says Pria.

"No...let's be unicorns flying through the sky!" Ella says.

"I want to be warriors too," Devon says. Ella doesn't think that's as fun...

...but she doesn't want to waste time arguing either.

"Okay, we can play warriors," she says. "But can we play unicorns next time?"

Pria and Devon nod. Then they team up to defend the castle together.

TAKING TURNS

If one of your friends always decides what games you play, try talking to them about taking turns. That way everyone will get a chance to do their favorite thing.

**Friends try not to interrupt or butt in,
and they respect personal space.**

Asha, Zoe and Maryam are at dance class, and the teacher tells
them to get into rows. Asha really wants to be beside her friends,
who are busy talking. She tries to wiggle in between them...

...but she can tell she's in the way. Instead she lines up in the front row.

"Great work," says the teacher during warm-up, so Asha feels okay about it after all.

BEING APART

A normal part of friendship is having to let go at certain times. It's not always easy in those moments, but it's okay! Good friends are always waiting for you afterward.

Do any of these examples feel familiar to you? Could you be a better friend if you keep these responses in mind? Which ones seem the most important? Are there any others you would add?

Remember that while you're trying your best, your friends are doing the same thing. And even though nobody's perfect, and you might have ups and downs, you'll always be there for one another.

Good friendships make everything better.
A great friend helps others be great!

AUTHOR'S NOTE

After working with children for close to 30 years, I have come to understand the tremendous importance of friendship in children's lives and overall development. Positive social interactions are a powerful protective factor for children—they can bounce back from setbacks or trauma more easily if they have dependable social connections. However, social skills don't always come naturally, and this is what inspired me to write *The Friendship Guide* as a resource for kids needing help. I hope readers find this book useful, feel more confident in being the best friends they can be and can look forward to a lifetime of strong and wonderful friendships.

FRIENDSHIP ACTIVITIES

Here are a few activities to help kids build and grow their friendships.

In the Classroom

- **Name Bingo:** Create bingo cards with the names of everyone in class (instead of numbers) and a small space beneath each to add notes. Give one to each student. Ask them to find the people named on their card and write down one fun fact about them. When they make a row of five, they have bingo!

- **Scavenger Hunt:** To promote teamwork, organize a scavenger hunt in which children work in pairs or small groups to find hidden objects.

- **Compliment Circle:** Have each child take a turn sitting in the center of a circle while the others give them compliments. This helps boost self-esteem and encourages positive interactions.

- **Cooperative Storytelling:** Sit in a circle and start a story. Have each child take a turn adding a sentence or two to the tale. This activity encourages listening and can lead to some very funny results!

At Home

- **Friendship Bracelets:** For a playdate, gather materials like beads, strings and charms so kids can make friendship bracelets together. When they're done, they can exchange bracelets.

- **Art Collaboration:** Provide a large piece of paper and art supplies, then ask siblings or friends to create a picture together. Creativity and cooperation are a great match.

- **Cooking Together:** Have children work together to prepare simple snacks or treats. Cooking fosters teamwork, and afterward they can taste together the results of their efforts.

- **Gratitude Journal:** To promote positive thinking, encourage children to keep a gratitude journal in which they write or draw things that they appreciate about their friends.

To my best friend, my sister Kellee: This book is
a thank you for all the laughs and adventures.
Here's to the magic of our friendship. —J.R.

For my friend Mildred. —A.A

Published in Canada and the United States in 2025 by Orca Book Publishers.
orcabook.com

Library and Archives Canada Cataloguing in Publication
Title: The friendship guide / Jillian Roberts ; illustrated by Andrea Armstrong.
Names: Roberts, Jillian, 1971– author. | Armstrong, Andrea, illustrator.
Identifiers: Canadiana (print) 20240341805 | Canadiana (ebook) 20240341813 | ISBN 9781459839311 (hardcover) |
ISBN 9781459839328 (PDF) | ISBN 9781459839335 (EPUB)
Subjects: LCGFT: Picture books.
Classification: LCC HQ784.F7 R63 2025 | DDC j302.34083—dc23

Library of Congress Control Number: 2024934928

Summary: In this sweet picture book, respected child psychologist Jillian Roberts outlines the key building blocks of being a good friend. From welcoming newcomers to being patient and kind, this book will help set up readers for a lifetime of wonderful friendships.

Orca Book Publishers is committed to reducing the consumption of nonrenewable resources in the production of our books. We make every effort to use materials that support a sustainable future.

Orca Book Publishers gratefully acknowledges the support for its publishing programs provided by the following agencies: the Government of Canada, the Canada Council for the Arts and the Province of British Columbia through the BC Arts Council and the Book Publishing Tax Credit.

Artwork created digitally.

Cover and interior artwork by Andrea Armstrong.
Design by Rachel Page.
Edited by Sarah Howden.

Printed and bound in South Korea.

28 27 26 25 • 1 2 3 4

Dr. Jillian Roberts is a child psychologist, author, professor at the University of Victoria and mother of three children. Considered a go-to child psychology expert for journalists, Dr. Roberts is a contributor to the *Globe and Mail*, *Global News* and CBC. She is the author of two bestselling and award-winning series of children's books: Just Enough and The World Around Us. Dr. Roberts' most recent titles, *Calm* and *My Promise*, are for the very youngest of readers and focus on building child resilience. She lives in Victoria, British Columbia.

Andrea Armstrong is a visual artist living in Vancouver, British Columbia. She spends her days (and often nights) illustrating, painting and designing. With roots in rural Indonesia, small-town Manitoba and metropolitan Singapore, she finds inspiration in the gathered impressions of her childhood. She holds a bachelor's degree in visual communications from Capilano University.